Parents Your
Children
Need You

Ife Doyin

WESTBOW
PRESS®
A DIVISION OF THOMAS NELSON
& ZONDERVAN

WestBow Press books may be ordered through booksellers or by contacting:

WestBow Press
A Division of Thomas Nelson & Zondervan
1663 Liberty Drive
Bloomington, IN 47403
www.westbowpress.com
1 (866) 928-1240

ISBN: 978-1-9736-0075-6 (sc)
ISBN: 978-1-9736-0074-9 (e)

Print information available on the last page.

WestBow Press rev. date: 10/19/2017

Dedication

This book is dedicated to my Lord and Saviour JESUS CHRIST who paid the price for my victory.

He Did It All for Me

For me He came, for me He gave
For me He was treated like a slave
He paid the price I could not pay
He poured His soul out, that day
Instead of poverty, I have prosperity
Instead of grief, I have joy and peace
Instead of shame, I have honour and dignity
Instead of death, I have life and ease
He paid for me to have His Name
Willingly went through sorrow and pain
He did it all for me!

By Ife Doyin

To my Children, Ope- you are now a beautiful young woman, strong and resilient in your faith. You are not only my daughter; you are my friend, sister and confidant.

Seun – my darling daughter, I have watched you growing into a fine young lady with great fortitude and grace. You are indeed my friend, my sister and my girl.

Ayo – son, you are worth more to me than ten sons. I look at you and I say to myself, Thank you JESUS!

And

To my lovely grandchildren, the Princess and the Lady. You have brought so much joy to our family.

When a baby is born, a star is born
A canvas on which we can form
Parents are the artists
who with some practice
will wield the Word
to paint on the board
Take heed how you paint
For this is a life that is born of LIGHT.

By Ife Doyin

Acknowledgement

I thank my darling sister Kemi for her love and support to me and especially to my children. I love you dearly Kemi.

I also wish to acknowledge my other siblings – Titi, Bimbo, Kunbi and Olugbo. I love you all.

To mummy, the woman who bore us all, may you long enjoy the fruit of your labour.

Foreword

When my mother asked me to write the foreword to her book, I was honored. I was honored, yet I knew I was one of three people most qualified to do so. For my mother has loved us with a love so true, so pure and so determined. As I have grown into adulthood and become a mother myself, I understand more and more the purpose and power of a mother's love. It was a mother's love that God had in mind in trying to describe the perfection of his own faithfulness.

Isaiah 49:15; Amplified Bible (AMP)
" [And the Lord answered] Can a woman forget her nursing child, that she should not have compassion on the son of her womb? Yes, they may forget, yet I will not forget you"

Wow! What a privilege to be used as an image to help the world understand God's heart and mind for us.

Parent's, it's this heart that made you open this book. It is the familiar desire for the success and wellbeing of your children that will keep you turning every page. I can relate to the determination to be the number one external influence for good in your children's lives that will take you to your knees and look to Heaven, as you connect with the words, scriptures and testimonies in this book.

My earliest memories are of my mother praying for me and my siblings. Because every thing she said was a prayer. She was always careful and purposeful with her words towards us, her words were always positive and affirming. Now looking back I know that she couldn't have always felt good and there must have been times when she was fearful or unsure. But she channelled these feelings into her prayers to the One who could change circumstances.

She has always believed that In spite of the challenges of today's world and for those wanting to love Christ; In spite of tragedies which many have faced; and even in spite of a rebellion which has threatened or threatens to shake your faith, hope and love to nothing - there is truly nothing that prayer and standing on God's Word cannot change.

She knows that neither a parent, nor his or her love is perfect, just as that scripture implies. However, I know that it is my mother's prayers that have preserved me from the one who seeks to steal, kill and destroy in this world. And I am grateful that she has carried on her mission with her grandchildren as well as empowering me to do the same for them and those to come.

So, I hope you take the lessons in this book and to heart. Whatever challenges you face as a parent, whatever obstacles you feel unfit to overcome, take them to the heart of God. He can never forget you. And your children need you.

Chapter One

Parents Your Children Need You

Parents this book comprises of the promises of God for your children which you can wield as confessions, declarations and prayers to keep them in God's will.

We are living in the era of which our children desperately need our help in prayers.

Yes, it is very good to give a good education but what would determine their success in life is not necessarily a good academic education; it is how much we are prepared to invest in their spiritual lives. How ready we are to water the seeds of greatness God has put in them with prayer.

I recall the day I was reflecting on 'life' and I heard God speak to my heart saying something like this....*you are your children's intercessor.* Before then, I had made it a point of praying for my children on a regular basis but when God spoke to me, it totally changed my perspective on my role in their lives. Suddenly, I realised the mandate of God's expectation for me to pray for my children. I had a responsibility to help shape their destinies with my prayers.

I was accountable for their destinies! This radicalised my prayers for my children.

I am sure you would agree with me that the world is a more dangerous place than it was when we were growing up. The devil's time is running out and he knows it. This is not the time to ostracise or yell and scream at them. It is not the time to tell everyone who comes into your home about how 'badly behaved your children are (or child is)' neither is it the time to lash out angrily or say words you will regret later.

The truth of the matter is that they are facing different demons, different challenges and different dangers from the ones we faced when growing up. There are 'Internet demons', 'peer pressure' demons, drugs demons, television demons… and a whole lot more. Our adversary is much organised in his onslaught on the people of God (especially children) in these times. He incorporates the method of 'catch them young' with the negative influence from magazines and peer pressure etc.

We need to ask ourselves, are we feeding our children with the Word? Are we diligent in our prayers for them and with them? On the other hand, are we leaving it to someone else, some educational institution or their peers? Are we leaving it to the internet, television or the world as a whole? Life does not just happen, life should be lived on purpose, with focus and determination to fulfil destiny.

We have a responsibility to our children to intercede for them. We need to join them on the 'war-front' or battlefield and wrestle with the enemy with them and on their behalf.

For we do not wrestle against flesh and blood, but against principalities, against powers, against the rulers of the darkness of this age, against spiritual hosts of wickedness in the heavenly places.

Ephesians 6:12 (NKJV)

It is our God-given responsibility which if not obeyed will have consequences not only on them but also on us, others, our communities, our nations and even the world.

Parents arise and intercede for your children regardless of their age; it does not matter if they are 4 or 40!

Chapter Two

Parent's Responsibilities

Your main responsibilities to your children are:

1. To bless them

In **Genesis 49: 1-2 & 8-28 (NIV)** we see where Jacob (Israel) gathered his children to himself before he died and blessed them.

Then Jacob called for his sons and said; "Gather around so I can tell you what will happen to you in days to come. "Assemble and listen, sons of Jacob; listen to your father Israel... ***(Verses 1 & 2) NIV***

Judah, your brothers will praise you;
your hand will be on the neck of your enemies;
your father's sons will bow down to you.
You are a lion's cub, Judah;
you return from the prey, my son.
Like a lion he crouches and lies down,

Like a lioness—who dares to rouse him?
  The sceptre will not depart from Judah,
  nor the ruler's staff from between his feet,
  until he to whom it belongs shall come
  and the obedience of the nations shall be his.
  He will tether his donkey to a vine,
    his colt to the choicest branch;
    he will wash his garments in wine,
    his robes in the blood of grapes.
    His eyes will be darker than wine,
    his teeth whiter than milk.

"Zebulun will live by the seashore
  and become a haven for ships;
  his border will extend toward Sidon.

"Issachar is a raw-boned donkey
  lying down among the sheep pens.
  When he sees how good is his resting place
  and how pleasant is his land,
  he will bend his shoulder to the burden
  and submit to forced labour.

"Dan will provide justice for his people
  as one of the tribes of Israel.
  Dan will be a snake by the roadside,
  a viper along the path
  that bites the horse's heels
  so that its rider tumbles backward.
  "I look for your deliverance, LORD.

"Gad will be attacked by a band of raiders,
but he will attack them at their heels.
"Asher's food will be rich;
he will provide delicacies fit for a king.

"Naphtali is a doe set free
that bears beautiful fawns.

"Joseph is a fruitful vine,
a fruitful vine near a spring,
whose branches climb over a wall.
With bitterness archers attacked him;
they shot at him with hostility.
But his bow remained steady,
his strong arms stayed limber,
because of the hand of the Mighty One of Jacob,
because of the Shepherd, the Rock of Israel,
because of your father's God, who helps you,
because of the Almighty, who blesses you
with blessings of the skies above,
blessings of the deep springs below,
blessings of the breast and womb.
Your father's blessings are greater
than the blessings of the ancient mountains,
than the bounty of the age-old hills.
Let all these rest on the head of Joseph,
on the brow of the prince among his brothers.

"Benjamin is a ravenous wolf;
in the morning he devours the prey,

in the evening he divides the plunder."

All these are the twelve tribes of Israel, and this is what their father said to them when he blessed them, giving each the blessing appropriate to him.

(Verses 8 – 28) NIV

The importance of calling your children and pronouncing blessings over them (*on purpose*) cannot be over emphasised.

As you decree blessings over them, you are actually re-aligning their lives to the Master plan (God's plans and purposes for them). You are exercising your kingdom authority by mandating divine alignment and it will happen.

You shall also decide *and* decree a thing, and it shall be established for you; and the light [of God's favour] shall shine upon your ways.

Job 22:28Amplified Bible (AMP)

"For the word of a king is authority *and* power, and who can say to him, what are you doing"

Ecclesiastes 8:4Amplified Bible (AMP)

It is also vital that they hear you bless them as it will increase their faith and self-esteem as we know that according to:

Romans 10:17;

"So then faith comes by hearing, and hearing by the word of God".

As parents, it is very important to agree with God on everything He spoke in His Word about our children. God has already said that His Word would accomplish, in:

Isaiah 55 verses 10 – 11 (NKJV)
"For as the rain comes down, and the snow from heaven,
And do not return there,
But water the earth,
And make it bring forth and bud,
That it may give seed to the sower
And bread to the eater,
So shall My word be that goes forth from My mouth;
It shall not return to Me void,
But it shall accomplish what I please,
And it shall prosper in the thing for which I sent it.

I remember when my, now grown up son, was a young boy, as I would lay hands on his head to bless him, he would kneel in front of me and tilt his head to me to receive the blessing. There was a morning, I think we were in a hurry and I omitted to do this, he reminded me by saying, *my blessing, you have not blessed me this morning,* or something to that effect.

2. Teach them the Word

Then the LORD *said, "Shall I hide from Abraham what I am about to do? Abraham will surely become a great and powerful nation, and all nations on earth will be blessed through him. For I have chosen him, so that he will direct His children and his household after him to keep the way of the* LORD *by doing what is right and just, so that the LORD will bring about for Abraham what he has promised him."*

Genesis 18 17-19 (NIV)

"Only be careful, and watch yourselves closely so that you do not forget the things your eyes have seen or let them fade from your heart as long as you live. Teach them to your children and to their children after them."

Deuteronomy 4:9 (NIV)

" These commandments that I give you today are to be on your hearts. Impress them on your children. Talk about them when you sit at home and when you walk along the road, when you lie down and when you get up"

Deuteronomy 6:6-7 (NIV)

God was confident that Abraham would teach his children (about Him) and so the Blessing would be generational, which was his intention. Likewise, God is relying on you to teach your children. In every home there should be a time and place for the family to meet for worship, study and pray together.

This is the family altar where they meet with God as a family. When this is an established function in a family, the children would learn to reverence God as God.

"Train up a child in the way he should go, And when he is old he will not depart from it"

Proverbs 22:6 (NKJV)

"And you, fathers, do not provoke your children to wrath, but bring them up in the training and admonition of the Lord."
Ephesians 6:4 (NKJV)

When children are taught the Word, they are enabled to know God themselves. The seeds of the Word sown by parents might not be evident immediately but it will grow and yield fruit eventually.

It's like having a rope tied to their feet, no matter how far out (into the world) they go, the Holy Spirit will 'reel' them in, in due time. Personally, I am seeing some seeds which I had sown into the lives of my children years ago taking root and yielding fruit now.

Children are also very perspective in that they watch what you do and not what you say. Your actions speak louder than what you say. **Ephesians 6.4** *says, not to provoke our children*, this means, do not say one and do another.

Do not try to force the Word down their throats, so to say, when you are not practising what you are preaching. This can lead to rebellion on the part of the children and you losing your respect with them. It might cause them to be angry thereby leaving them with the impression that Christians are hypocrites. They might falsely assume all Christians to be like that.

This is very dangerous because it will give them a false picture of what the Body of Christ stands for and how the church should function. For example, there was a time when I was in a church and some of the children were a bit rude. I found out that their parents were discussing matters about other members of the church in their presence and this initiated a lot of gossip among the children and a lack of respect for leadership. It was not fair on the children as they were not to blame.

Unfortunately, the consequences of things like this can be far influencing, the children could actually have a tainted image of people in church and believe that the church is pretentious. What a way to grow up!

"A good man leaves an inheritance [of moral stability and goodness] to his children's children, and the wealth of the sinner [finds its way eventually] into the hands of the righteous, for whom it was laid up"
Proverbs 13:22Amplified Bible (AMP)

A good inheritance includes a wealth of knowledge and understanding of the Word of God. I told my children that if all I left them was a very sound grasp of who God is, who they are in Christ and the importance of prayer and an intimate relationship with God, then I have left them everything. Of course, I will leave my properties, investments and so on, but the greatest investment I will leave them is the Word.

Dear parents, God refers to someone who leaves an inheritance for his children and children's children as a good man.

He who spares his rod hates his son, but he who loves him disciplines him promptly
Proverbs 13:24(NKJV)

The Bible says that parents who do not discipline their children hate them. This might seem a bit harsh to some but it is the truth. Notice that, 1 Corinthians 13:6 says that; "*Love does not rejoice in iniquity but rejoices in the truth (NKJV)*" if we do not discipline (correct) our children accordingly then, we are not demonstrating love to them.

Part of parental discipline is to train a child in the Word of Righteousness and as a disciple of Jesus.

We can speak faith-filled and power-filled words over our children. The force of faith will actually cause our words to act as projectiles and conform their lives to what we say. Too much emphasis cannot be laid on the fact that we must speak **THE WORD** only.

Confess and decree the Blessing:

I declare and decree that my children are blessed in their going out and coming. In. They are at the top in honour and at the top in power; they are at the top spiritually, academically, socially, financially and physically.

I declare and decree that the paths of my children are cleared to the top by the superior blood of Jesus and I forbid any evil to befall them.

I declare and decree that the paths of my children are shining brighter and brighter unto the full day.

I declare and decree that every hindrance to their advancement is pulled down, dismantled, shattered and aborted. I cut my children off from every evil family flow and I turn back every familiar spirit in our family bloodline from operating in their lives.

I declare and decree that my children are for signs and wonders and they begin to manifest in miracles, greatness and prominence. The seed of greatness in them flourishes, germinates, takes root and explodes into glory.

I declare and decree that the safety of God is around my children and the fire of divine security is upon them.

I declare and decree that they are comfortable and excel with ease in life. It is easy for my children: academically, financially, in ministry and in their marriages. It is easy! It is easy! It is easy!

I declare and decree that they walk fully pleasing to God and that God rejoices over them with clapping and singing.

I declare and decree that my children understand God as their God and not only as their parents' God.

I declare and decree that my children become an eternal excellence and a joy of many generations.

I declare and decree that my children exercise kingdom dominion and inherit the earth.

I declare and decree that the earth yield its goodness to my children and they will long enjoy the work of their hands.

I declare and decree that my children be willing and obedient to God therefore they eat the goodness of the land.

I declare and decree that my children wax stronger and stronger in the grace of giving.

I declare and decree that my children possess the gates of their enemies.

I declare and decree that my children be taught by the Lord with great reward for their well-being.

I declare and decree that my children inherit the earth.

I declare and decree that my children serve God in spirit and in truth

3. Send the Word

"He sent His Word and healed them, and delivered them from their destructions".
Psalm 107:20 (NKJV)

"It is the Spirit who gives life; the flesh profits nothing. The words that I speak to you are spirit, and they are life"
John 6:63 (NKJV)

" In the beginning was the Word, and the Word was with God, and the Word was God."
John 1:1 (NKJV)

Parents can send the Word as a projectile into the lives of their children. The Word is power-filled and if mixed with faith will hit the target every-time. The Word is filled with life and it execute the purpose of which it is sent speedily

Is not my Word like fire and like a hammer, which goes forth and breaks in pieces the rocks?
Jeremiah 23: 29 (NKJV)

You can send the Word to your children no matter where they are, no matter the situation and no matter the challenges they face. The Word has the ability to break or shatter every evil or obstacle.

The Lord will give strength to His people; The Lord will bless His people with peace.

Psalm 29:11 (NKJV)

I send the strength of God into my children now! Let the strength of God enter their hearts, their bodies and the situation they are facing now.

I pronounce the blessing of the peace of God on my children today. I release the peace of God into their hearts and decree that their hearts be enveloped in the peace of God.

For I, says the Lord, will be a wall of fire all around her, and I will be the glory in her midst.

Zechariah2:5 (NKJV)

I release the fire of God around my children to surround and protect them from evil.

Let the glory of God be upon my children and repel every demoniac and diabolical persons from them.

You will arise and have mercy and loving-kindness for Zion, for it is time to have pity and compassion for her; yes, the set time has come [the moment designated].

Psalm 102:13Amplified Bible (AMP)

Lord, have mercy on my children.
The favour of God surrounds my children like a shield.

Gates

Lift up your heads, O you gates; and be lifted up, you age-abiding doors, that the King of glory may come in.

Who is the King of glory? The Lord strong and mighty, the Lord mighty in battle.

Lift up your heads, O you gates; yes, lift them up, you age-abiding doors that the King of glory may come in.

Who is [He then] this King of glory? The Lord of hosts, He is the King of glory. Selah [pause, and think of that]!
Psalm 24:7-10 Amplified Bible (AMP)

I will break down gates of bronze and cut through bars of iron.
Isaiah 45:2 (NIV)

Prayer: Let the every gate of brass (difficulty, challenges) before my children be shattered to pieces.

And I also say to you that you are Peter, and on this rock I will build my church, and the gates of Hades shall not prevail against it
Matthew 16:18 (NKJV)

The gates of hell shall not prevail against my children.

'For I will defend this city, to save it For My own sake and for my servant David's sake.'
2 kings 19:34 (NKJV)

Let the gates of their lives be fortified and defended by the Lord of hosts.

This Word was what I received from God when one of my children was facing a challenge in the University. As I took and held on to this scripture, the situation changed in my child's favour.

A negatively written decision that the faculty had made was changed to my child's favour. God is good to us all the time.

Therefore your gates *shall be open continually; They shall not be shut day or night, That men may bring to you the wealth of the Gentiles, And their kings in procession*
Isaiah 60:11 (NKJV)

Let the gates of my children be opened day and night and the nations bring their wealth to them, with their kings in procession

The angel of the Lord encamps all around those who fear Him, and delivers them.
Psalm 34:7 (NKJV)

Let the gates of the lives of my children be guarded by the Angel of the Lord

Turn away my eyes from looking at worthless things, And revive me in Your way. Establish your word to your servant, who is devoted to fearing you. Turn away my reproach, which

I dread, for your judgements are good. Behold, I long for your precepts; Revive me in your righteousness.

Psalm 119:37- 40 (NKJV)

Let their eyes and ears of understanding be receptive only to righteousness and holiness.

Release angels:

But, to which of the angels has He ever said; Sit at My right hand until I make your enemies your footstool. Are they not all ministering spirits sent forth to minister for those who will inherit salvation?

Hebrews 1:13-14 *(NKJV)*

For He shall give His angels charge over you, to keep you in all your ways.

Psalm 91:1 (NKJV)

Turn away my eyes from beholding vanity (idols and idolatry); and restore me to vigorous life and health in your ways.

Establish your word and confirm your promise to your servant, which is for those who reverently fear and devotedly worship you.

Turn away my reproach, which I fear and dread, for your ordinances are good.

Behold, I long for your precepts; in your righteousness give me renewed life.

Psalm 103:20 – 21 (AMP)

Bless (affectionately, gratefully praise) the Lord, you His angels, you mighty ones who do His commandments, hearkening to the voice of His word.

Bless (affectionately, gratefully praise) the Lord, all you His hosts, you His ministers who do His pleasure.

Bless the Lord, all His works in all places of His dominion; bless (affectionately, gratefully praise) the Lord, O my soul!

Angels are waiting for instructions to move into action on behalf of your children. There are delegated angels whose job is to protect your children, if you give the go -ahead.

Let the Angel of the Lord go before my children always.

I release the ministering spirits of God to surround my children and keep them from evil.

Let the angelic host bear my children up so they will not fail, fall or falter.

Angels of God I release you to work on behalf of my children to bring them into their divine purpose(s).

Let the angels of warfare fight for my children even when they do not know it.

Surely, goodness and mercy shall follow my children all the days of their lives.

I speak life

As we are made in the image of God, he has given us His power to speak life. In *Genesis chapter one* we see that God spoke creation into existence. He said 'Light be!' and there was light. He spoke light in the face of darkness. God has put in us the same power to speak life into existence. Speak life over your children. Do not be moved by what you see, what people are saying, or what the circumstances are like.

Speak life in the face of death.

Speak joy in the face of sorrow

Speak success in the face of failure

Speak victory in the face of defeat

Speak peace in the face of turmoil.

I call heaven and earth as witnesses today against you, that I have set before you; life and death, blessing and cursing; therefore choose life, that both you and your descendants may live;
Deuteronomy 30:19 (NKJV)

Jesus said to him, "I am the way, the truth, and the life. No one comes to the Father except through me.
John 14:6 (NKJV)

I speak life into every organ in my children's body (*Name the organs*)

I speak life into their God - ordained relationships

I speak life into their minds and intellect

I speak life into their future and destiny

I speak life into their zeal for God and knowing Him.

I choose life, I choose the blessing so my descendants, and me will live and not die.

Always plead the Blood of Jesus over your children.

When you do this, you are reinforcing the victory Jesus won for us in their lives. You are appropriating the victory in their lives. You are also letting Satan know he cannot touch them. The devil knows the power in the Blood, he knows he has no authority over the Blood of Jesus, he knows that he has been totally and eternally defeated by the Blood of Jesus. Do you know it?

I plead the Blood

Therefore, brethren, having boldness to enter the Holiest by the blood of Jesus,

Hebrews 10:19 (NKJV)

………….. To Jesus the Mediator of the new covenant and to the blood of sprinkling that speaks better things than that of Abel.

Hebrews 12:24 (NKJV)

And they overcame him by the blood of the Lamb and by the word of their testimony, and they did not love their lives to the death.

Revelation 12:11(NKJV)

I plead the Blood of Jesus over my children.

I plead the Blood of Jesus over their entire bodies, souls and spirits.

I plead the Blood of Jesus over their future, present and past.

I plead the Blood over their properties, their rooms and their friends.

I plead the Blood over their homes, relationships and education.

Let the paths of my children be cleared to the top by the Blood of Jesus.

I hold the Blood against every negative influence.

I hold the Blood of Jesus against peer pressure.

I hold the Blood of Jesus against failure.

I hold the Blood of Jesus against predators.

I hold the blood of Jesus against addiction (*name the addiction*).

I hold the Blood of Jesus against the spirit of this era.

I hold the Blood of Jesus against the spirit of rebellion.

I hold the Blood of Jesus against the spirit of death.

Outpouring of the Holy Spirit

For I will pour water on him who is thirsty, And floods on the dry ground; I will pour My Spirit on your descendants,

And my blessing on your offspring; They will spring up among the grass Like willows by the watercourses.' One will say, 'I am the Lord's'; Another will call himself by the name of Jacob;

Another will write with his hand, 'The Lord's,' And name himself by the name of Israel.

Isaiah 44:3-5 (NKJV)

Confession:

There is a continuous outpouring of the Spirit of God on the lives of my children. The Spirit of God causes my children to walk in wisdom and in reverential fear of God. They are therefore walking in the path of righteousness with understanding and making decisions that are fully pleasing to God. They are free from errors and mistakes that would jeopardise their destinies. They operate by the counsel of

God and are strong in the Lord and in the power of His might.

My children are filled with the knowledge of God and do not judge by the hearing of their ears but diligently follow God and seek His counsel continuously.

Covenant Promises for our children.

*Know therefore that the **Lord** your God, He is God, the faithful God, who keeps His covenant and His loving kindness to a thousandth generation with those who love Him and keep His commandments*

Deuteronomy 7:9 (NASB)

God is a Covenant – keeping God and this Covenant was cut between God (our Daddy) and Jesus (our Brother) on our behalf. The Blood of Jesus inaugurated this Covenant and it covers our children. When we pray let us have the confidence that every Word of promise that God made to us in the Word for our children is part of the covenant. Just as God swore and cut covenant with Abram *(Genesis 15: 17-18)* with the body and blood of animals so has God sworn and cut covenant with us through the Body and Blood of His Son JESUS CHRIST. The Word of God for our children are soaked Blood – soaked, Blood - inaugurated and Blood - fulfilling.

Holy Communion is a powerful way to activate this covenant in the lives of our children.

When we partake of the Holy Communion, let us meditate on the Word of promise (Covenant promise) and speak those words over the lives of our children, thank God because His promises for our children and us are 'yes and Amen' in Christ Jesus. This activates the covenant over their lives. What this does is place a demand on the Covenant and Praise God for the Covenant supplies in abundance every time.

"All your children will be taught by the LORD, and great will be their peace".

Isaiah 54:13 (NIV)

Here am I and the children whom the Lord has given me! We are for signs and wonders in Israel from the Lord of hosts, who dwells in Mount Zion

Isaiah 8:18 (NKJV)

And it shall come to pass in the last days, says God,
That I will pour out of My Spirit on all flesh; Your sons and your daughters shall prophesy, Your young men shall see visions, Your old men shall dream dreams

Acts 2:17 (NKJV)

Praise the Lord! Blessed is the man who fears the Lord,
Who delights greatly in His commandments? His descendants will be mighty on earth;

Psalm 112:1-2 (NKJV)

"Therefore know that the Lord your God, He is God, the faithful God who keeps covenant and mercy for a thousand generation with those who love Him and keep His commandments;

Deuteronomy 7:9 (NKJV)

Blessed shall be the fruit of your body, the produce of your ground and the increase of your herds, the increase of your cattle and the offspring of your flocks.
Deuteronomy 28:4 (NKJV)

Then she spoke out with a loud voice and said,
"Blessed are you among women, And blessed is the fruit of your womb!
Luke 1:42 (NKJV)

"For as the new heavens and the new earth, Which I will make shall remain before me," says the Lord, "So shall your descendants and your name remain?
Isaiah 66:22 (NKJV)

Fear not, for I am with you; I will bring your descendants from the east, And gather you from the west;
Isaiah 43:5 (NKJV)

I have been young, and now am old; Yet I have not seen the righteous forsaken, Nor his descendants begging bread
Psalm 37:25 (NKJV)

Below are specific concerns you might be having about your child/children. Please address these with the relevant prayers and the Word.

Prayers against addiction/rebellion/Infirmity and so on

Parents there are some situations that look impossible when viewed from the human standpoint. The first thing you want to do is to ask...why Lord? Then the next thing is to panic about how hopeless the situation looks. I know how that feels...I have been there. The truth is when our children hurt we hurt too. It is painful to watch your children in pain or hurting. Remember, God understands and he knows exactly how you feel. He had to go through that too when His Son, His only Son suffered and died for the sins of the whole world.

The first thing I recommend, is to take deep breaths and do not panic. Run to pick up your bible, open and pull covenant promises and write them down. I have given just a few in my book but the Word of God is filled with covenant promises for us and our children to our thousandth generation.

Therefore, I urge you, brothers and sisters, in view of God's mercy, to offer your bodies as a living sacrifice, holy and pleasing to God—this is your true and proper worship. Do not conform to the pattern of this world, but be transformed by the renewing of your mind. Then you will be able to test and approve what God's will is—his good, pleasing and perfect will.

Romans 12:1-2 (NIV)

Secondly, meditate on the covenant promises and let It saturate your mind and heart, remember the battle is in the mind. As you fill yourselves with the Word, faith is growing in your heart and you are being strengthened. You will notice that suddenly the problem is looking smaller ....smaller and God is looking bigger and bigger. Now, notice that I did not say God is getting bigger and bigger. God, our heavenly

Father is already the Almighty God and with Him all things are possible.

(Mark 10:27 NASB)

Thirdly, activate the covenant by partaking of Holy Communion. As you do this, visualise Jesus going to the cross to pay for your child's (children) lives. Visualise the chastening he received for the well-being of your child. Visualise every stripe he was beaten and his flesh torn apart in exchange for your child's addiction/sickness. Remember that somebody has paid the price and bought freedom for your child. Then with this conviction partake of Holy Communion and declare freedom for your child. This is the reality of the Gospel.

"Surely our griefs He Himself bore, And our sorrows He carried; Yet we ourselves esteemed Him stricken, Smitten of God, and afflicted.

But He was pierced through for our transgressions, He was crushed for our iniquities; The chastening for our well-being *fell* upon Him, And by His scourging we are healed"

Isaiah 53: 4 -5 (NASB)

Fourthly, pray in the Spirit. As we do not know exactly what the root cause of the situation/problem is, the best Person to help us pray for our children is the Holy Spirit. As a matter of fact, we should practice praying in the spirit every day not only when we have needs or are going through a hard situation.

Remember in Romans 8:26:

In the same way, the Spirit also helps our weakness; for we do not know how to pray as we should, but the Spirit Himself intercedes for *us* with groaning too deep for words; and He who searches the hearts knows what the mind of the Spirit is, because He intercedes for the saints according to *the will of* God

> ➢ *I decree that my child's body, soul and spirit solely belongs to Jesus Christ.*
> ➢ I saturate my child's body, soul and spirit in the Blood of Jesus.
> ➢ I command every onslaught/attack on his/her mind to be obliterated.
> ➢ I forbid mind-controlling demons to operate in my child's life.
> ➢ Satan you cannot have my child. In Jesus name.
> ➢ Satan, I command you to get your filthy hands off my child.
> ➢ I confess that my child daily presents his/her body to God as a living sacrifice, holy, acceptable to God which is his/her reasonable service.
> ➢ Let every battle in my child's mind be won by the Lord Jesus.
> ➢ I bind every demon of drug addiction working against my child.
> ➢ I release my child from the grip of mind controlling spirits.

- ➤ I wage war on every dark power waging war on my child's life and destiny.
- ➤ I superimpose the will of God over the will of the enemy in my child's life.
- ➤ I decree and declare that my child will fulfil divine destiny and purpose.
- ➤ My child will not go to hell.
- ➤ Let the desire for harmful substance/drugs be purged out by the fire of God.
- ➤ My child shall not die, but live to declare the works of the Lord.

For Academic Excellence

Whereas you have been forsaken and hated, so that no one went through you, I will make you an eternal excellence, a joy of many generations.

You shall drink the milk of the Gentiles, and milk the breast of kings; you shall know that I, the Lord, am your saviour and redeemer, the Mighty One of Jacob.

Instead of bronze, I will bring gold, Instead of Iron, I will bring silver, Instead of wood, bronze, and instead of stones, Iron. I will also make your officers peace, And your magistrates righteousness

Isaiah 60:15 - 17 (NKJV)

As for these four young men, God gave them knowledge and skill in all literature and wisdom; and Daniel had understanding in all visions and dreams.

Daniel 1:17 (NKJV)

And in all matters of wisdom and understanding about which the king examined them, He found them ten times better than all the Magicians and astrologers who were in all his realm.

Daniel 1:20 (NKJV)

I have more understanding than all my teachers, For Your testimonies are my meditation.

Psalm 119:99 (NKJV)

Prayers for academic excellence

I decree that the paths of my children are cleared to the top by the Blood of Jesus. They stand out in excellence amongst their peers and they bring joy to me and many generations. They are royal diadems in the Hand of God and are blessed and highly favoured.

I decree that my children are assets to their father/mother, cousins, their friends, schools, country and me. They are assets in the Body of Christ and are always above and never beneath. They have more knowledge than their teachers do as the Holy Spirit guides them into all truth and shows them things to come.

Instead of c's and d's they receive A's and B's,

Instead of failure, they receive success

Instead of stress and anxiety, they receive peace and calmness.

Instead of fear (of examinations), they receive faith and fortitude

Instead of frustration, they receive fulfilment.

Instead of defeat, they receive victory.

Instead of hardship, they receive ease.

Instead of timidity, they receive boldness.

Instead of inadequacy, they receive divine abilities

Instead of low self-esteem, they receive confidence

Instead of confusion, they receive clear understanding

Instead of regression, they receive progression

Prayer against negative influences or peer pressure.

Many parents know that peer pressure is one of the major ways in which some children get into trouble. It starts out with children trying to impress one another and then subtly negative behaviour in someone is seen as 'good' and 'popular'. The well behaved child becomes 'unpopular' and tries to win back the 'respect' of the group or 'friend' by giving in to negative or even destructive behaviour.

My son, if your heart is wise, my heart will be glad, even mine;

Yes, my heart will rejoice when your lips speak right things.

Let not your heart envy sinners, but continue in the reverent and worshipful fear of the Lord all the day long.

For surely there is a latter end [a future and a reward], and your hope and expectation shall not be cut off.

Hear, my son, and be wise, and direct your mind in the way [of the Lord].

Do not associate with winebibbers; be not among them nor among gluttonous eaters of meat,

For the drunkard and the glutton shall come to poverty, and drowsiness shall clothe a man with rags.

Hearken to your father, who begot you, and despise not your mother when she is old.

Buy the truth and sell it not; not only that, but also get discernment and judgment, instruction and understanding.

The father of the [uncompromisingly] righteous (the upright, in right standing with God) shall greatly rejoice, and he who becomes the father of a wise child shall have joy in him.

Let your father and your mother be glad, and let her who bore you rejoice.

My son, give me your heart and let your eyes observe and delight in my ways

Proverbs 23:15-26 Amplified Bible (AMP)

Prayers

I nullify every negative influence over my children's lives.

I separate my children from every person that God has not planted. In their lives.

I dismantle every hindrances and satanic blockages to my children's progress in life.

Holy Spirit, please saturate the lives of my children with your anointing.

I decree that my children belong to God and nothing can separate them from His Love.

My children are inscribed on the palm of God's hand and their walls are forever before Him.

They will hear the voice of the Holy Spirit without interference and the voice of a stranger they will not obey.

I declare that like Jesus, my children walk and operate

according to the volume of the book God have written concerning them.

I call forth every resources and assistance my children need to fulfil divine purpose and destiny.

My children will never beg for bread and would never lack anything good.

Doors of favour will open of their own accord, for my children.

O Lord, let your mercy speak saturate the lives of my children all their days.

Prayer for protection

> *Build a wall of prayer around your children. You cannot be with them 24/7 but your prayers can.*

> *The name of the Lord is a strong tower; the righteous run to it and are safe.*
> ### *Proverbs 18:10 (NKJV)*

Father, I run into your Name with my children. I thank you that your Name is a strong tower and your safety surrounds us.

Please pray **Psalm 91** *over your children constantly:*

Psalm 91 Amplified Bible (AMP)

1. He who dwells in the secret place of the Most High shall remain stable *and* fixed under the shadow of the Almighty [Whose power no foe can withstand].

2. I will say of the Lord, He is my Refuge and my Fortress, my God; on Him I lean *and* rely, *and* in Him I [confidently] trust!

3. For [then] He will deliver you from the snare of the fowler and from the deadly pestilence.

4. [Then] He will cover you with His pinions, and under His wings shall you trust *and* find refuge; His truth *and* His faithfulness are a shield and a buckler.

5. You shall not be afraid of the terror of the night, nor of the arrow (the evil plots and slanders of the wicked) that flies by day,

6. Nor of the pestilence that stalks in darkness, nor of the destruction *and* sudden death that surprise *and* lay waste at noonday.

7. A thousand may fall at your side, and ten thousand at your right hand, but it shall not come near you.

8. Only a spectator shall you be [yourself inaccessible in the secret place of the Most High] as you witness the reward of the wicked.

9. Because you have made the Lord your refuge, and the Most High your dwelling place,

10. There shall no evil befall you, nor any plague *or* calamity come near your tent.

11. For He will give His angels [especial] charge over you to accompany *and* defend *and* preserve you in all your ways [of obedience and service].

12. They shall bear you up on their hands, lest you dash your foot against a stone.

13. You shall tread upon the lion and adder; the young lion and the serpent shall you trample underfoot.

14. Because he has set his love upon Me, therefore will I deliver him; I will set him on high, because he knows *and* understands My name [has a personal knowledge of My mercy, love, and kindness—trusts and relies on Me, knowing I will never forsake him, no, never].

15. He shall call upon Me, and I will answer him; I will be with him in trouble, I will deliver him and honor him.

16. With long life, will I satisfy him and show him My salvation.

Beloved parents,

This is just a guideline that you can use as a framework to build on.

Always speak the Word over your children, agree with God's Word concerning your children.

Do not allow your feelings to get in the way of your praying and believing God about your children.

Put your emotion under so you can see the way forward for your children, ***no matter how bad the situation looks.***

Pray without ceasing............

1 Thessalonians 5:17 (NKJV)

Printed in the United States
By Bookmasters